Race Cars
on the Go

by Beth Bence Reinke

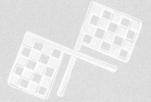

BUMBA BOOKS™

LERNER PUBLICATIONS ◆ MINNEAPOLIS

Note to Educators:

Throughout this book, you'll find critical thinking questions. These can be used to engage young readers in thinking critically about the topic and in using the text and photos to do so.

Lerner Publications Company
A division of Lerner Publishing Group, Inc.
241 First Avenue North
Minneapolis, MN 55401 USA

For reading levels and more information, look up this title at www.lernerbooks.com.

Library of Congress Cataloging-in-Publication Data

Names: Reinke, Beth Bence, author.
Title: Race cars on the go / Beth Bence Reinke.
Description: Minneapolis : Lerner Publications, [2018] | Series: Bumba books. Machines that go | Carefully leveled text and fresh, vibrant photos engage young readers in learning about how race cars work. Age-appropriate critical thinking questions and a photo glossary help build nonfiction learning skills"--Provided by publisher. | Includes bibliographical references and index. | Audience: Age 4-7. | Audience: K to grade 3.
Identifiers: LCCN 2017012901 (print) | LCCN 2017030245 (ebook) | ISBN 9781512482591 (eb pdf) | ISBN 9781512482508 (lb : alk. paper)
Subjects: LCSH: Automobiles, Racing--Juvenile literature. | Racetracks (Automobile racing)--Juvenile literature.
Classification: LCC TL236 (ebook) | LCC TL236 .R445 2018 (print) | DDC 629.228/5--dc23

LC record available at https://lccn.loc.gov/2017012901

Manufactured in the United States of America
2-52501-33119-1/21/2022

Expand learning beyond the printed book. Download free, complementary educational resources for this book from our website, www.lernerresource.com.

Table of
Contents

Race Cars

Race cars go fast.

They have powerful

engines.

These engines give

them speed.

A driver controls the car.

The driver sits in the cockpit.

The steering wheel turns the car.

Foot pedals make the car stop and go.

There are many kinds

of race cars.

Stock cars look like

regular cars.

The tires are under the car.

How are stock cars different from regular cars?

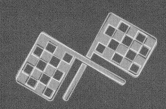

Some race cars have tires on the

outside of the main body.

These cars are called

open-wheel cars.

An open-wheel race car does not have a roof.

The driver's head sticks out.

Why do you think a race car driver wears a helmet?

Dragsters have long,

thin bodies.

They are the fastest

race cars.

What other machines are long?

Many race cars race on tracks.

They make laps around a track.

Some race cars make pit stops during a race. The crew puts on new tires. They fill the car with more gas too.

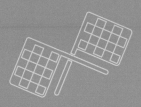

Race cars zoom across the finish line.

Do you want to drive a race car?

Parts of a Race Car

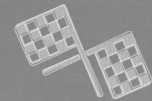

cockpit

roof

steering
wheel

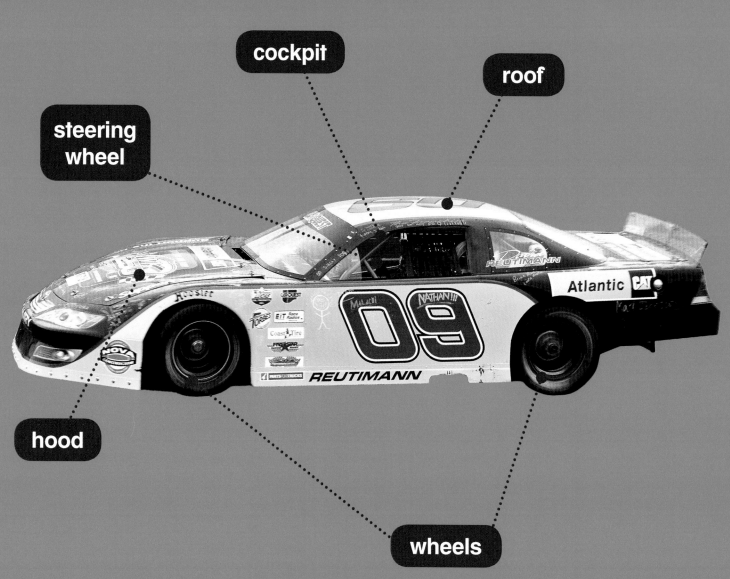

hood

wheels

Picture Glossary

cockpit

where the driver sits to control the race car

engines

machines that give race cars their power

laps

trips around a racetrack

pit stops

quick breaks

Read More

Silverman, Buffy. *How Do Formula One Race Cars Work?* Minneapolis: Lerner Publications, 2016.

Tuchman, Gail. *Race Day.* Washington, DC: National Geographic, 2010.

West, David. *Race Cars.* Mankato, MN: Smart Apple Media, 2016.

Index

Photo Credits

The images in this book are used with the permission of: © Action Sports Photography/Shutterstock.com, pp. 4–5, 6, 17, 23 (top left), 23 (bottom left); © Daniel Hurlimann/Shutterstock.com, pp. 8–9, 18–19, 23 (bottom right); © HodagMedia/Shutterstock.com, pp. 11, 13; © Joshua Rainey Photography/Shutterstock.com, pp. 14–15; © ARprofessionals.com.my/Shutterstock.com, pp. 20–21; © Matthew Jacques/Shutterstock.com, p. 22; © Sjoerd van der Wal/iStock.com, p. 23 (top right).

Front Cover: © avid_creative/iStock.com.